Copyright © 2023 by Michael Jaynes (Author)

This book is protected by copyright law and is intended solely for personal use. Reproduction, distribution, or any other form of use requires the written permission of the author. The information presented in this book is for educational and entertainment purposes only, and while every effort has been made to ensure its accuracy and completeness, no guarantees are made. The author is not providing legal, financial, medical, or professional advice, and readers should consult with a licensed professional before implementing any of the techniques discussed in this book. The content in this book has been sourced from various reliable sources, but readers should exercise their own judgment when using this information. The author is not responsible for any losses, direct or indirect, that may occur from the use of this book, including but not limited to errors, omissions, or inaccuracies.

We hope this book has been informative and helpful on your journey to understanding and celebrating older adults. Thank you for your interest and support!

Title: The Battle Rages On
Subtitle: Sports' Most Intense Feuds Continue

Series: Red War Rivalries: The Evolution and Impact of Sports' Greatest Feuds
By Michael Jaynes

"Liverpool against Manchester United is probably one of the most intense rivalries in football history."
Steven Gerrard, former Liverpool captain

"The rivalry between Liverpool and Manchester United is steeped in history, and it's something that every player wants to be a part of."
Rio Ferdinand, former Manchester United defender

"It's the greatest rivalry in sports, in my opinion. When you think about the history, the passion, the intensity, it's unmatched."
Alex Rodriguez, former Yankee player

"There's just something about playing the Yankees that brings out the best in the Red Sox, and vice versa. It's a special feeling."
Dustin Pedroia, former Red Sox player

"The Celtics-Lakers rivalry is the best in all of sports."
Bill Simmons

"It's always special when the Celtics and Lakers play. The history, the tradition, the excellence of both franchises, it's all there."
Larry Bird

"The McLaren-Ferrari rivalry was so intense because they were two of the biggest and most successful teams in Formula One history. They were always pushing each other to the limit, both on and off the track."
Martin Brundle, former Formula One driver and commentator

Table of Contents

Introduction 7
- *The Media's Role in Fueling Rivalries* 7
- *Fan Culture and Red War Rivalries* 10
- *The Evolution of Red War Competitions* 13
- *The Globalization of Red War Rivalries* 15
- *The Future of Red War Rivalries in the Age of Technology* 17

Chapter 1: New York Yankees vs. Boston Red Sox in Baseball 20
- *Origins of the Rivalry* 20
- *Key Players and Memorable Moments* 23
- *The Curse of the Bambino and Its Legacy* 26
- *Recent Matchups and Future Prospects* 29
- *The Impact of the Rivalry on the American League* 31

Chapter 2: Brazil vs. Argentina in Soccer 33
- *Origins of the Rivalry* 33
- *Key Players and Memorable Matches* 36
- *Cultural Significance of the Rivalry* 38
- *Recent Matchups and Future Prospects* 40
- *The Role of National Identity in the Rivalry* 43

Chapter 3: Armstrong vs. Ullrich in Cycling 46
- *Origins of the Rivalry* 46

    Key Races and Memorable Moments *49*

    Doping Scandals and the Legacy of the Rivalry *52*

    The Importance of the Tour de France in the Rivalry *55*

Chapter 4: Ohio State vs. Michigan in College Football **58**

    Origins of the Rivalry *58*

    Key Players and Memorable Moments *61*

    The Impact of the Rivalry on College Football *65*

    Recent Matchups and Future Prospects *68*

    The Role of Coaches in the Rivalry *71*

Conclusion **74**

    The Evolution of Red War Rivalries in Sports *74*

    The Importance of Fans and Media in Fostering Rivalries *77*

    The Future of Red War Rivalries in a Changing Sports Landscape *80*

    The Impact of Globalization on Red War *83*

Key Terms and Definitions **86**

Supporting Materials **88**

Introduction

The Media's Role in Fueling Rivalries

Sports rivalries are not just about the players and the teams. They are also about the fans, the media, and the culture surrounding the sports. In many cases, sports rivalries are created and fueled by the media, which has the power to shape public perception and influence the way people think about sports and their favorite teams. In this chapter, we will explore the role of the media in fueling sports rivalries and the impact it has on the sports industry and society.

The Power of the Media

The media, including television, radio, newspapers, and social media, has a significant impact on the way we experience sports. It shapes our perceptions of the teams, players, and events, and can even create or amplify rivalries. The media has the power to frame a narrative and influence the way people think about a particular team or player. For example, if the media portrays a team as the underdog, it can create sympathy and support among fans, which can fuel a rivalry if the opposing team is seen as the favorite.

The Media's Role in Creating Rivalries

In some cases, the media creates rivalries out of thin air. For example, the media may hype up a matchup between two teams or players who have no history of animosity, but simply because it makes for good television or generates clicks and views online. The media may also manufacture controversies or conflicts between players or teams to create a storyline for a game or season.

The Media's Role in Amplifying Rivalries

While some rivalries may be created by the media, others already exist and are amplified by the media. The media coverage of a rivalry can increase the intensity and passion of the fans, which in turn can fuel the rivalry even further. The media may also focus on the negative aspects of a rivalry, such as trash-talking or physical altercations, which can create a perception that the rivalry is more heated than it actually is.

The Impact of Media-Fueled Rivalries

Media-fueled rivalries can have both positive and negative impacts on the sports industry and society. On one hand, they can generate interest and excitement among fans, which can lead to increased ticket sales, TV ratings, and revenue for the teams and the league. Rivalries can also create a sense of community and identity among fans, who feel a strong connection to their favorite team and its history.

On the other hand, media-fueled rivalries can also create a toxic and divisive atmosphere, where fans become hostile and aggressive towards each other. This can lead to violence and vandalism, and can even spill over into other areas of society. The media has a responsibility to report on sports in a fair and accurate way, and not to create or amplify rivalries that could have negative consequences.

Conclusion

The media plays a crucial role in shaping our perceptions of sports and creating or amplifying rivalries. While some rivalries may be organic and natural, others are created or amplified by the media for the sake of entertainment or profit. As sports continue to evolve in the age of technology and social media, the media's role in fueling rivalries will only become more important. It is up to the media to use this power responsibly and to ensure that sports rivalries do not become toxic or harmful to society.

Fan Culture and Red War Rivalries

Sports rivalries are not just about the players and the teams. They are also about the fans and the culture surrounding the sports. In many cases, sports rivalries are driven by the passion and loyalty of the fans, who take great pride in their favorite teams and their history. In this chapter, we will explore the role of fan culture in fueling sports rivalries, and how it has shaped the sports industry and society.

The Importance of Fan Culture

Fan culture is a critical component of sports. Fans bring energy and enthusiasm to the games, create traditions and rituals, and foster a sense of community and identity around their favorite teams. Fans are also the ones who create and sustain rivalries, as they develop a deep-seated dislike for opposing teams and their fans. In many cases, rivalries between teams are fueled by the passion and loyalty of the fans, who take great pride in their team's history and accomplishments.

The Evolution of Fan Culture

Fan culture has evolved over time, from simple cheering and chanting to more elaborate and sophisticated forms of expression. Today, fans have access to a wide range of tools and technologies to express their love for their teams and to taunt their rivals, including social media, online forums, and mobile apps. Fan culture has also become more commercialized, as teams and leagues have recognized the value of selling merchandise and creating fan experiences that go beyond the game itself.

The Role of Fan Culture in Red War Rivalries

Fan culture plays a critical role in fueling red war rivalries, as fans are often the ones who create and sustain the animosity between teams. Fans engage in trash-talking, taunting, and even violence to show their support for their team and their disdain for their rivals. This behavior can create a toxic and divisive atmosphere, where fans become hostile and aggressive towards each other. Red war rivalries can also be fueled by cultural and political differences between the teams, as well as historical events that have shaped the relationship between the teams and their fans.

The Impact of Red War Rivalries on Fan Culture

Red war rivalries can have both positive and negative impacts on fan culture. On one hand, rivalries can create a sense of community and identity among fans, who feel a strong connection to their favorite team and its history. Rivalries can also generate excitement and interest in the games, leading to increased attendance, TV ratings, and revenue for the teams and the league. On the other hand, rivalries can create a toxic and divisive atmosphere, where fans become hostile and aggressive towards each other, leading to violence and vandalism.

The Future of Fan Culture and Red War Rivalries

As sports continue to evolve in the age of technology and social media, the role of fan culture in fueling red war rivalries will only become more important. Teams and leagues will need to find ways to harness the passion and loyalty of the fans, while also ensuring that rivalries do not become toxic or harmful to society. This will require a balance between commercial interests and the integrity of the sport, as well as a commitment to promoting sportsmanship and respect among fans.

Conclusion

Fan culture is a critical component of sports, and plays a crucial role in fueling red war rivalries. While rivalries can generate excitement and interest in the games, they can also create a toxic and divisive atmosphere that is harmful to society. As sports continue to evolve, it will be important for teams and leagues to find ways to harness the passion and loyalty of the fans, while also promoting sportsmanship and respect among fans. Only then can red war rivalries continue to thrive in a way that is both entertaining and responsible.

The Evolution of Red War Competitions

Red war competitions have evolved significantly over time, with changes in technology, globalisation, and the culture of sports. From the early days of sports, rivalries have been a key component of the competitive landscape, with fans and players alike engaging in heated battles on and off the field. As sports have grown in popularity and reach, these rivalries have become even more intense, fuelled by the media and the passion of fans around the world.

One significant change in the evolution of red war competitions has been the increased professionalisation of sports. As sports have become more organised and commercialised, the stakes have become higher, with more money and prestige on the line. This has led to more intense rivalries and a greater focus on winning at all costs.

Another factor in the evolution of red war competitions has been the rise of technology. With the advent of television, social media, and other forms of digital communication, rivalries have taken on a new dimension, with fans and players alike able to connect with each other and engage in heated debates and discussions.

Globalisation has also had a significant impact on the evolution of red war competitions. As sports have become more global, with fans and players from around the world participating, rivalries have become more complex and diverse, with cultural and national identities playing an increasingly important role.

In addition to these external factors, the evolution of red war competitions has also been shaped by changes in the culture of sports. As fans have become more passionate and engaged, rivalries have become more intense and emotional, with fans often identifying closely with their favourite teams and players.

Overall, the evolution of red war competitions has been shaped by a complex interplay of factors, including professionalisation, technology, globalisation, and changes in the culture of sports. While the nature of these rivalries has changed over time, they remain a key component of the competitive landscape, with fans and players alike continuing to engage in heated battles on and off the field.

The Globalization of Red War Rivalries

The globalization of red war rivalries has been one of the most significant developments in the world of sports in recent years. As sports have become more global in nature, with players and fans from around the world participating in events, rivalries have taken on a new dimension, with cultural and national identities playing an increasingly important role.

One of the most significant examples of the globalization of red war rivalries is the rivalry between Brazil and Argentina in soccer. This rivalry has deep cultural roots, with both countries seeing soccer as a key part of their national identity. As a result, matches between the two teams are always highly anticipated, with fans around the world tuning in to watch the action.

Another example of the globalization of red war rivalries is the rivalry between the New York Yankees and the Boston Red Sox in baseball. While this rivalry has its roots in the United States, it has become a global phenomenon, with fans around the world tuning in to watch the two teams battle it out on the field.

The globalization of red war rivalries has also been facilitated by advances in technology. With the rise of social media and other forms of digital communication, fans around the world are able to connect with each other and engage in heated debates and discussions about their favourite teams and players. This has helped to fuel the intensity of red war rivalries, with fans around the world feeling a sense of connection and solidarity with their fellow supporters.

In addition to these external factors, the globalization of red war rivalries has also been driven by changes in the culture of sports. As sports have become more commercialized and professionalized, rivalries have taken on a new dimension, with more money and prestige on the line. This has led to greater intensity and passion among players and fans alike, with the stakes of these rivalries higher than ever before.

Overall, the globalization of red war rivalries has been a significant development in the world of sports, with cultural and national identities playing an increasingly important role in these heated battles. As sports continue to become more global in nature, it is likely that these rivalries will only become more intense and meaningful, with fans around the world tuning in to watch their favourite teams and players battle it out on the field.

The Future of Red War Rivalries in the Age of Technology

The future of red war rivalries in the age of technology is a topic of great interest and speculation in the world of sports. As technology continues to evolve at a rapid pace, it is likely that red war rivalries will be impacted in a variety of ways, from the way fans engage with the sport to the way athletes train and compete.

One of the most significant ways that technology is likely to impact red war rivalries is through the rise of new media platforms. Social media, streaming services, and other digital platforms have already had a profound impact on the way fans engage with sports, and this is likely to continue in the years ahead. As more fans turn to these platforms to watch matches and connect with other fans, it is likely that red war rivalries will take on a new dimension, with fans around the world able to engage in heated debates and discussions in real-time.

Another way that technology is likely to impact red war rivalries is through advances in training and performance analysis. From wearable technology to data analytics, there are a wide range of tools available to athletes and coaches to help them improve their performance on the field. As these tools become more sophisticated and widely available, it is likely that athletes will be able to gain an edge over their rivals, leading to even more intense and exciting battles on the field.

At the same time, technology is likely to pose some challenges for red war rivalries in the years ahead. One of the biggest concerns is the potential for performance-enhancing drugs and other forms of cheating. As technology continues to advance, it is likely that new forms of doping and other illicit activities will emerge, posing a significant threat to the integrity of sports.

Another potential challenge for red war rivalries in the age of technology is the risk of overcommercialization. As sports become more commercialized and corporate, there is a risk that the passion and intensity of red war rivalries could be lost. Fans may become disillusioned with the sport if they feel that it is being driven purely by profit motives, rather than a genuine love of the game.

Despite these challenges, however, there is much to be excited about in the future of red war rivalries. As technology continues to evolve, it is likely that we will see new and innovative ways for fans to engage with sports and for athletes to train and compete. Whether it is through new media platforms, cutting-edge training techniques, or other advances, the future of red war rivalries is sure to be an exciting and dynamic one.

Chapter 1: New York Yankees vs. Boston Red Sox in Baseball

Origins of the Rivalry

The rivalry between the New York Yankees and the Boston Red Sox is one of the most storied and intense in all of sports. This rivalry has its roots in the early days of baseball and has continued to evolve over the years, with each team vying for supremacy in the American League.

The origins of the rivalry can be traced back to the early 20th century, when both teams were relatively new to the American League. The Red Sox were founded in 1901, while the Yankees were established in 1903 as the Baltimore Orioles before relocating to New York the following year. In the early days of their rivalry, the two teams were fairly evenly matched, with both winning their fair share of games against each other.

However, the rivalry truly began to take shape in the 1920s, when the Yankees began to establish themselves as one of the premier teams in baseball. Led by the legendary Babe Ruth, the Yankees won their first World Series championship in 1923 and would go on to win several more over the next decade. The Red Sox, meanwhile, struggled to keep pace with their rivals from New York, failing to win a championship during this period.

Despite the Yankees' dominance, the Red Sox were still able to put up a fight and occasionally come out on top in head-to-head matchups. One of the most memorable moments in the early history of the rivalry came in 1919, when the Red Sox sold Babe Ruth to the Yankees in what would later be known as the "Curse of the Bambino." Many Red Sox fans believed that the team's failure to win a championship in the years following the trade was due to a curse placed on the team as a result of their decision to sell Ruth to the Yankees.

Throughout the 20th century, the rivalry continued to grow and evolve. Both teams saw periods of success and failure, with each looking to gain the upper hand in their head-to-head matchups. Some of the most memorable moments in the history of the rivalry include the "Bloody Sock" game in the 2004 American League Championship Series, when Red Sox pitcher Curt Schilling famously pitched with a bloody sock and led his team to victory over the Yankees. The Red Sox would go on to win their first World Series championship in 86 years that year, breaking the so-called "Curse of the Bambino" that had plagued the team for decades.

Today, the rivalry between the Yankees and the Red Sox remains as strong as ever. Both teams continue to compete at a high level, and each game between the two teams is hotly contested. Whether it's the historic stadiums, the passionate fan bases, or the storied histories of both franchises, there is no denying that the rivalry between the Yankees and the Red Sox is one of the most intense and enduring in all of sports.

Key Players and Memorable Moments

The Yankees-Red Sox rivalry has seen numerous players on both sides who have made significant contributions to the rivalry's history. From Babe Ruth to Derek Jeter, and from Ted Williams to David Ortiz, these players have left an indelible mark on this storied rivalry.

One of the most iconic players in the history of the rivalry is Babe Ruth. Ruth started his career with the Red Sox in 1914 and helped lead them to three World Series championships in 1915, 1916, and 1918. However, in 1920, Red Sox owner Harry Frazee sold Ruth to the Yankees, and the rest, as they say, is history. Ruth went on to become one of the greatest players in baseball history and helped lead the Yankees to four World Series championships in the 1920s.

Another player who played a significant role in the rivalry is Ted Williams. Williams played his entire career with the Red Sox from 1939 to 1960 and is widely regarded as one of the greatest hitters of all time. Williams had numerous memorable moments in the rivalry, including hitting a walk-off home run in the final game of the 1949 season to clinch the batting title over Yankees outfielder Joe DiMaggio.

In more recent years, players like Derek Jeter and David Ortiz have become synonymous with the rivalry. Jeter played his entire career with the Yankees from 1995 to 2014 and helped lead them to five World Series championships. He also had numerous clutch moments in the rivalry, including hitting a walk-off home run in Game 4 of the 2004 American League Championship Series against the Red Sox.

Ortiz, on the other hand, played for the Red Sox from 2003 to 2016 and was a key player in the team's three World Series championships in 2004, 2007, and 2013. He had numerous clutch hits against the Yankees in his career, including a walk-off home run in Game 4 of the 2004 ALCS and a game-tying grand slam in Game 2 of the 2013 ALCS.

Other players who have left their mark on the rivalry include Roger Clemens, Pedro Martinez, and Mariano Rivera. Clemens played for both the Red Sox and the Yankees and had some memorable moments against both teams. Martinez, on the other hand, played for the Red Sox from 1998 to 2004 and had numerous dominant performances against the Yankees, including striking out 17 batters in a game in 1999.

Rivera, perhaps the greatest closer of all time, played his entire career with the Yankees from 1995 to 2013 and had numerous clutch moments against the Red Sox in his career. He famously closed out Game 7 of the 2003 ALCS against the

Red Sox with three scoreless innings to send the Yankees to the World Series.

Overall, the Yankees-Red Sox rivalry has seen numerous key players who have made significant contributions to the rivalry's history. From Babe Ruth to David Ortiz, these players have left an indelible mark on this storied rivalry, and their performances will be remembered by fans for generations to come.

The Curse of the Bambino and Its Legacy

The Curse of the Bambino is one of the most infamous legends in the history of baseball. It refers to the alleged curse that was placed upon the Boston Red Sox franchise following the trade of Babe Ruth to the New York Yankees in 1919. The Curse is said to have lasted for 86 years, during which time the Red Sox experienced a string of heartbreaking losses, including multiple World Series defeats.

Origins of the Curse

The story of the Curse of the Bambino begins in 1919 when Babe Ruth, a talented but controversial player, was sold to the New York Yankees by Red Sox owner Harry Frazee for a sum of $125,000. At the time, the Red Sox were a successful franchise, having won five World Series titles in the previous 15 years. However, they had failed to win a championship since 1918, and Frazee was in need of cash to finance a new Broadway play he was producing.

The trade was controversial from the outset, with many Red Sox fans outraged that their team would part with such a talented player. The Boston Globe ran a headline that read, "No Money in the Treasury to Buy Babe Ruth," reflecting the sentiment of many fans.

The Curse Takes Hold

The Red Sox did not win another championship until 2004, a span of 86 years that came to be known as the Curse of the Bambino. During this time, the team suffered a series of heartbreaking losses, including four World Series defeats in which they held a lead in the deciding game. In 1946, they lost to the St. Louis Cardinals in Game 7 of the World Series, despite being up by a run in the eighth inning. In 1967, they lost to the Cardinals again, this time in Game 7 of the World Series after leading the series three games to one. In 1975, they lost to the Cincinnati Reds in Game 7 of the World Series, despite being up 3-0 in the sixth inning.

As the years went on, the Curse of the Bambino became a cultural phenomenon, with fans and media alike attributing the team's lack of success to the trade of Babe Ruth. Many believed that the curse was real, and that the Red Sox would never win a championship until it was broken.

Breaking the Curse

The Curse of the Bambino finally came to an end in 2004, when the Red Sox won their first World Series championship since 1918. The team's victory was seen as a triumph over the curse, and it was celebrated by fans across the country. The Red Sox went on to win two more championships in the next decade, cementing their status as one of the most successful franchises in baseball.

Legacy of the Curse

The Curse of the Bambino may have been a legend, but it had a very real impact on the Boston Red Sox franchise. For decades, the team struggled to win championships and was often seen as a symbol of futility. However, the curse also served to unite fans and players alike, creating a sense of camaraderie and resilience that ultimately led to the team's success in breaking it.

Today, the Curse of the Bambino is remembered as a cautionary tale about the dangers of trading away talented players, and as a testament to the power of belief and perseverance in the face of adversity.

Recent Matchups and Future Prospects

In recent years, the rivalry between the Yankees and the Red Sox has continued to produce some of the most exciting and high-stakes matchups in baseball. Both teams have made significant moves to bolster their rosters and compete for championships.

The 2018 season saw the Red Sox dominate the American League, finishing with a league-best 108 wins and capturing their fourth World Series title in 15 years. The Yankees, on the other hand, finished the regular season with 100 wins, the third-highest total in baseball, but fell to the Red Sox in the American League Division Series.

In 2019, the Yankees and Red Sox continued to compete at a high level, with the Yankees finishing with 103 wins, the second-highest total in baseball, and the Red Sox finishing with 84 wins, just missing out on a playoff spot. The two teams split their season series, with each winning 10 games.

Looking to the future, both the Yankees and Red Sox have reason for optimism. The Yankees have a young core of talented players, including Aaron Judge, Gleyber Torres, and Luis Severino, and have made significant additions to their pitching staff, signing Gerrit Cole to a record-breaking contract in the 2019 offseason. The Red Sox, meanwhile, still have a strong nucleus of players, including Xander Bogaerts and Rafael Devers, and have a new manager in Alex Cora, who led the team to its 2018 World Series championship.

Off the field, both teams continue to be among the highest-spending in baseball, with the Yankees and Red Sox consistently ranking among the top teams in payroll. This financial commitment ensures that both teams will continue to be competitive and will have the resources to make moves to improve their rosters.

While it's impossible to predict the future of the rivalry with certainty, one thing is for sure: the Yankees and Red Sox will continue to be among the most talented and competitive teams in baseball. With their shared history, passionate fan bases, and intense desire to win, the rivalry between these two teams will continue to be one of the most captivating and exciting in all of sports.

The Impact of the Rivalry on the American League

The rivalry between the New York Yankees and Boston Red Sox has had a significant impact not only on the teams involved, but also on the American League as a whole. The intense competition between the two teams has fueled interest in the league and drawn in fans from all over the country.

One of the most significant impacts of the rivalry has been the boost in television ratings and attendance numbers. When the Yankees and Red Sox play each other, it's not just another game – it's a spectacle. Fans flock to the stadium, and millions tune in to watch the game on TV. This surge in interest has had a ripple effect, leading to higher advertising revenue, increased merchandise sales, and a general boost in the league's profile.

The rivalry has also had an impact on other teams in the American League East. With the Yankees and Red Sox consistently vying for the top spot in the division, other teams have had to step up their game to compete. This has led to a more competitive and exciting division overall, as each team strives to topple the perennial powerhouses.

Beyond the financial and competitive impacts, the rivalry has also had a cultural impact on the American League. The rivalry has become a part of the league's identity, with fans and players alike recognizing the importance and intensity of the matchup. The rivalry has produced iconic moments and legendary players, from Babe Ruth and Ted Williams to Derek Jeter and David Ortiz.

As the league moves forward, the rivalry between the Yankees and Red Sox will undoubtedly continue to be a major force. Both teams have strong rosters and passionate fan bases, ensuring that each matchup will be must-see TV. The rivalry will continue to drive interest in the league and push teams to new heights.

Chapter 2: Brazil vs. Argentina in Soccer
Origins of the Rivalry

The rivalry between Brazil and Argentina is one of the most intense and storied in the world of soccer. It is a rivalry that dates back over 100 years, with roots that go beyond just sport. To understand the origins of this rivalry, we must look at the history of these two countries and the socio-political factors that have shaped their relationship over time.

The first soccer match between Brazil and Argentina took place on July 20, 1914, in Buenos Aires. At the time, soccer was still a relatively new sport in South America, but it was quickly gaining popularity. The match between Brazil and Argentina was seen as an opportunity to showcase the sport and the talent of the two countries.

The match ended in a 3-0 victory for Argentina, but it was not the scoreline that would come to define the rivalry. Rather, it was the atmosphere in the stadium that set the tone for future encounters. The fans were passionate and vocal, and tensions between the two sets of supporters ran high.

As soccer grew in popularity in both countries, the rivalry between Brazil and Argentina became more intense. The two nations began to dominate the sport in South America, and their matches became more frequent and more significant. The rivalry took on a life of its own, fueled by national pride and a desire to prove superiority on the soccer field.

However, the rivalry between Brazil and Argentina goes beyond just soccer. The two countries have a long and complex history, marked by periods of cooperation and conflict. In the early 20th century, both countries were emerging as major powers in South America, and there was a sense of competition between them for regional influence.

This competition was exacerbated by political differences. Brazil was a federal republic, while Argentina was a centralized government. These different political systems created tensions between the two countries and contributed to the rivalry on the soccer field.

The rivalry between Brazil and Argentina continued to grow throughout the 20th century, with memorable matches and moments that are still talked about today. The 1978 World Cup final, which saw Argentina defeat the Netherlands to win their first world title, is one of the most iconic moments in soccer history. The 1990 World Cup round of 16 match, which saw Argentina defeat Brazil 1-0, is another memorable moment in the history of the rivalry.

Today, the rivalry between Brazil and Argentina remains as intense as ever. The two nations continue to dominate soccer in South America, and their matches are eagerly anticipated by fans around the world. While the origins of the rivalry may be rooted in history, its legacy is one of the greatest rivalries in the world of sport.

Key Players and Memorable Matches

Brazil and Argentina are two of the most successful soccer nations in history, and their fierce rivalry on the pitch has produced some of the most memorable matches in the sport. The rivalry between Brazil and Argentina can be traced back to the early 20th century, and over the years, it has evolved into one of the most intense and passionate rivalries in world football.

One of the earliest and most significant matches between the two sides took place in the 1937 South American Championship, which was held in Argentina. In the final of the tournament, Brazil defeated Argentina 2-0 in front of a hostile Buenos Aires crowd. The match was marked by violent incidents on and off the field, and the Brazilian players were attacked by the Argentine fans.

Another memorable match between the two sides took place in the 1978 World Cup, which was hosted by Argentina. Brazil, who were one of the favorites to win the tournament, faced Argentina in the second round, and the match ended in a 0-0 draw. However, the game was marred by controversy, as the Brazilian striker Zico had a goal disallowed for a dubious offside decision.

In recent years, Brazil and Argentina have faced each other in several high-profile matches, including in the Copa

America and World Cup qualifiers. One of the most memorable matches between the two sides in recent times was the 2004 Copa America final, which was held in Peru. In the final, Brazil defeated Argentina 4-2 on penalties after a thrilling 2-2 draw in regulation time. The match was marked by some outstanding individual performances, with Brazilian striker Adriano scoring two goals and Argentine playmaker Juan Roman Riquelme providing two assists.

Other memorable matches between the two sides include the 1990 World Cup Round of 16 match, which Argentina won 1-0 thanks to a goal from Claudio Caniggia, and the 2018 World Cup Round of 16 match, which saw a masterful performance from Argentine superstar Lionel Messi, who scored one goal and provided two assists in a 4-3 victory over Brazil.

Overall, the rivalry between Brazil and Argentina has produced some of the most exciting and dramatic matches in soccer history. The two sides are among the most successful nations in the sport, and their clashes on the pitch always produce high drama and intense emotions. Whether in World Cups, Copa Americas, or friendly matches, the rivalry between Brazil and Argentina continues to captivate soccer fans around the world.

Cultural Significance of the Rivalry

The rivalry between Brazil and Argentina in soccer is not just a competition on the field, but a reflection of the cultural and historical differences between the two countries. From language to politics to cuisine, Brazil and Argentina have distinct identities that shape the way their citizens view each other and their soccer teams.

Language is a key factor in the cultural differences between Brazil and Argentina. While Portuguese is the official language of Brazil, Spanish is the dominant language in Argentina. This language barrier can make it difficult for fans and players from the two countries to communicate effectively, leading to misunderstandings and tensions both on and off the field.

Politics also play a role in the cultural significance of the Brazil-Argentina rivalry. The two countries have a history of political and economic competition, with Brazil being the larger and more influential of the two. This dynamic is reflected in their soccer matches, with each team representing their country's power and prestige on the international stage.

Food and drink are another aspect of the cultural differences between Brazil and Argentina. Brazil is known for its barbecue (churrasco) and traditional drinks like caipirinha, while Argentina is famous for its beef and wine. These culinary differences are reflected in the food and drink consumed by fans at soccer matches, with each country's cuisine representing a point of pride and identity.

The cultural significance of the Brazil-Argentina rivalry is also reflected in the media coverage of their soccer matches. Brazilian and Argentine journalists often use nationalistic language and imagery to describe the games, framing them as battles between two proud and distinct cultures. This type of coverage can fuel nationalist sentiment and contribute to tensions between the two countries.

Overall, the cultural differences between Brazil and Argentina make their soccer rivalry more than just a game. The language barrier, political and economic competition, culinary differences, and media coverage all contribute to a sense of national pride and identity that fuels the passion and intensity of their matches.

Recent Matchups and Future Prospects

The Brazil vs. Argentina rivalry is one of the oldest and most intense rivalries in the world of soccer. The two teams have faced each other over 100 times since their first match in 1914, with each team having their share of victories and defeats. In this chapter, we will examine some of the recent matchups between these two teams and discuss their future prospects.

Recent Matchups

In recent years, Brazil and Argentina have faced each other several times in various international tournaments, including the Copa America, World Cup qualifiers, and friendly matches. One of the most memorable recent matchups between these two teams was the final of the 2021 Copa America, which was held at the Maracanã Stadium in Rio de Janeiro, Brazil. The match was closely contested, with Argentina scoring the only goal of the game in the 22nd minute. This victory marked Argentina's first major trophy in 28 years, and it was particularly satisfying for their captain, Lionel Messi, who had previously lost four finals with the national team.

Another notable recent matchup between Brazil and Argentina was the semi-final of the 2019 Copa America, which was held in Brazil. In that match, Brazil defeated

Argentina 2-0, with goals from Gabriel Jesus and Roberto Firmino. This victory helped Brazil to reach the final of the tournament, which they went on to win.

In addition to these two matches, Brazil and Argentina have faced each other several times in World Cup qualifiers in recent years. The most recent match was in November 2021, which ended in a 1-1 draw. These matches are always hotly contested, as both teams are determined to qualify for the World Cup and prove their dominance in South American soccer.

Future Prospects

Looking ahead, the future prospects for Brazil and Argentina in soccer are bright, and it is likely that these two teams will continue to be major players on the international stage. Both teams have a rich history of producing talented players who have gone on to achieve great success at the club and international level.

One of the key factors that will shape the future of this rivalry is the emergence of new talent. Both Brazil and Argentina have a strong tradition of developing young players, and it is likely that we will see many new stars emerge in the coming years. Players like Neymar, Gabriel Jesus, and Richarlison have already made a name for themselves on the Brazilian side, while Argentina has produced players like Lionel Messi, Sergio Agüero, and Paulo Dybala.

Another factor that will impact the future of this rivalry is the changing landscape of international soccer. The COVID-19 pandemic has disrupted the schedules of many tournaments and has led to changes in the format of some competitions. Additionally, the upcoming World Cup in Qatar in 2022 will be the first to be held in November and December, which may have an impact on the scheduling of international matches.

In conclusion, the rivalry between Brazil and Argentina in soccer is one of the most intense and passionate rivalries in the world of sports. Both teams have a long history of success and are likely to continue to be major players on the international stage for years to come. With the emergence of new talent and the changing landscape of international soccer, the future of this rivalry is sure to be full of exciting matches and memorable moments.

The Role of National Identity in the Rivalry

The Brazil vs. Argentina soccer rivalry is one of the most intense and long-standing rivalries in the world of sports. While the on-field battles between these two soccer powerhouses are well-documented, the rivalry extends far beyond the pitch. This chapter will explore the role of national identity in the Brazil vs. Argentina soccer rivalry and how it has helped to shape the intensity and passion of this fierce competition.

Historical Context:

The Brazil vs. Argentina soccer rivalry dates back to the early 1900s, and it has been shaped by historical and cultural factors. Brazil was a Portuguese colony until it gained independence in 1822, while Argentina was a Spanish colony until it declared independence in 1816. The two countries have a long history of political and economic competition, which has spilled over into their sporting rivalry. Soccer became a popular sport in both countries in the early 1900s, and it was only a matter of time before Brazil and Argentina would face off on the soccer field.

National Identity:

National identity plays a significant role in the Brazil vs. Argentina soccer rivalry. The rivalry is not just a battle between two soccer teams; it is a battle between two nations.

The two countries have different cultures, languages, and histories, which have helped to shape their distinct national identities. Brazil is known for its vibrant and colorful culture, while Argentina is known for its passion and intensity. These cultural differences have helped to fuel the rivalry and have made it one of the most intense in the world of sports.

The rivalry is also fueled by the fact that both countries take great pride in their soccer teams. Soccer is the national sport of both Brazil and Argentina, and winning the World Cup is seen as the ultimate achievement. The two countries have won a combined nine World Cup titles, and both are perennial contenders in every major international soccer tournament. The rivalry between Brazil and Argentina is not just about winning a soccer match; it is about national pride and identity.

On-Field Battles:

The Brazil vs. Argentina soccer rivalry has produced some of the most memorable matches in the history of the sport. The on-field battles between these two teams are often heated and physical, with both sides determined to come out on top. The rivalry has produced some of the greatest soccer players in history, including Pele, Diego Maradona, and Lionel Messi.

One of the most memorable matches in the Brazil vs. Argentina soccer rivalry took place in the 1990 World Cup in Italy. Brazil and Argentina faced off in the round of 16, with Brazil winning 1-0. The match was a classic example of the intensity and passion of the rivalry, with both sides giving their all on the field.

Future Prospects:

The Brazil vs. Argentina soccer rivalry is showing no signs of slowing down, and it is likely to continue to be one of the most intense and passionate rivalries in the world of sports. Both countries have strong soccer programs and a deep pool of talented players, which means that the rivalry is likely to remain highly competitive for years to come.

Conclusion:

National identity plays a significant role in the Brazil vs. Argentina soccer rivalry. The rivalry is not just a battle between two soccer teams; it is a battle between two nations. The cultural differences between Brazil and Argentina have helped to fuel the intensity and passion of the rivalry, and both countries take great pride in their soccer teams. While the on-field battles between these two teams are often heated and physical, the rivalry extends far beyond the pitch and has helped to shape the identity of both nations.

Chapter 3: Armstrong vs. Ullrich in Cycling
Origins of the Rivalry

The rivalry between Lance Armstrong and Jan Ullrich is one of the most significant and controversial in the history of cycling. The two athletes faced off in some of the most challenging races in the world, including the Tour de France, and their competition captivated fans around the globe. However, the rivalry was not just about competition between two elite athletes. It also represented larger cultural and social forces that shaped cycling during the 1990s and early 2000s.

The origins of the Armstrong-Ullrich rivalry can be traced back to the early 1990s, when both athletes were starting their professional careers. Armstrong, a young and talented American cyclist, quickly gained attention for his aggressive riding style and his determination to succeed. Ullrich, a young German cyclist, was also making waves in the sport, demonstrating his strength and endurance in a variety of races.

Their paths first crossed at the 1996 Olympic Games in Atlanta, where Armstrong won the bronze medal in the individual time trial and Ullrich won the gold. However, it was not until the Tour de France in 1999 that their rivalry truly began to take shape.

Armstrong had won the Tour de France the previous year, but Ullrich was considered his main rival for the title. The two athletes battled it out over the grueling 21-stage race, with Armstrong ultimately emerging as the winner. However, Ullrich was not deterred and continued to challenge Armstrong in subsequent years, finishing second to Armstrong in the Tour de France three times between 2000 and 2003.

The rivalry between Armstrong and Ullrich was not just about competition on the road, however. It also represented a larger cultural clash between American and European cycling styles. Armstrong was known for his aggressive and dominant approach, while Ullrich was known for his more reserved and calculated style. This clash between different cycling cultures only added to the drama and excitement of their competition.

In addition, the rivalry between Armstrong and Ullrich was shaped by the larger social and cultural forces that were impacting cycling during this time period. The 1990s and early 2000s were a time of significant change and upheaval in the sport, with the emergence of new technologies, doping scandals, and increased media scrutiny.

Armstrong and Ullrich were both impacted by these changes, and their rivalry took on a new significance in light of these larger cultural shifts. Armstrong's well-documented battle with cancer and his subsequent return to cycling also added to the drama of their competition, as did Ullrich's reputation as a formidable opponent who was willing to take risks to win.

Overall, the origins of the Armstrong-Ullrich rivalry can be traced back to the early 1990s, when two young and talented cyclists first began to make their mark on the sport. Their competition represented not just a battle between two elite athletes, but also a clash between different cycling cultures and larger social and cultural forces that were shaping the sport during this time period.

Key Races and Memorable Moments

The rivalry between Lance Armstrong and Jan Ullrich in cycling is one of the most memorable and controversial in the sport's history. The two cyclists competed against each other in numerous races throughout their careers, with each race adding to the intensity of the rivalry. In this section, we will explore the key races and memorable moments that helped shape the Armstrong-Ullrich rivalry.

Tour de France 2001

The 2001 Tour de France was a defining moment for both Armstrong and Ullrich. Armstrong had already won the previous two editions of the race, while Ullrich was considered his main rival. The two riders were closely matched throughout the race, with Armstrong taking the yellow jersey on stage 10 and holding onto it until the end. Ullrich finished in second place, just over six minutes behind Armstrong.

Tour de France 2003

The 2003 Tour de France saw Armstrong and Ullrich once again battling for the top spot. Ullrich was leading the race after the first time trial, but Armstrong managed to catch up and take the lead in the next stage. The two riders were neck-and-neck throughout the race, but Armstrong ultimately prevailed, winning his fifth Tour de France title.

Ullrich finished in second place, just over a minute behind Armstrong.

Tour de France 2004

The 2004 Tour de France was a rematch of sorts for Armstrong and Ullrich. Ullrich was determined to finally beat Armstrong and take the yellow jersey, while Armstrong was looking to win his sixth consecutive Tour de France title. The two riders were once again closely matched, but Armstrong managed to stay ahead of Ullrich, winning the race by a margin of just over six minutes.

Olympic Games 2000

The rivalry between Armstrong and Ullrich extended beyond the Tour de France. In the 2000 Olympic Games in Sydney, Australia, the two cyclists competed against each other in the time trial event. Ullrich was considered the favorite, having won the event in the previous Olympic Games. However, Armstrong managed to edge out Ullrich, winning the gold medal by just over two seconds.

Conclusion

The rivalry between Lance Armstrong and Jan Ullrich in cycling was one of the most intense and controversial in the sport's history. The two riders were closely matched and pushed each other to new heights in their respective careers. The key races and memorable moments they shared will be remembered for years to come, as they helped define an era of cycling that was both thrilling and controversial.

Doping Scandals and the Legacy of the Rivalry

The rivalry between Lance Armstrong and Jan Ullrich in professional cycling was one of the most intense and controversial in the history of the sport. While both cyclists achieved great success and amassed numerous accolades throughout their careers, their rivalry was ultimately overshadowed by a series of doping scandals that rocked the sport.

Origins of the Rivalry The rivalry between Armstrong and Ullrich can be traced back to the late 1990s, when both riders emerged as rising stars in the world of professional cycling. Armstrong, a young American cyclist, had overcome testicular cancer and returned to the sport with a newfound sense of purpose and determination. Ullrich, a talented rider from Germany, had already established himself as one of the top cyclists in the world, winning the Tour de France in 1997.

The two riders first faced off in the 1998 Tour de France, where Ullrich emerged as the overall winner and Armstrong finished a disappointing 36th. This initial defeat seemed to fuel Armstrong's drive and determination, and he returned to the race the following year with a renewed sense of purpose. In the years that followed, Armstrong and Ullrich would engage in a series of intense battles on the roads of

Europe, with each rider pushing themselves to the limit in pursuit of victory.

Key Races and Memorable Moments One of the most memorable moments in the Armstrong-Ullrich rivalry came in the 2001 Tour de France, when the two riders engaged in an epic battle on the slopes of the legendary Alpe d'Huez climb. Armstrong, riding with his trademark grit and determination, managed to pull away from Ullrich in the final kilometers of the stage, ultimately winning the race by just six seconds.

The following year, the two riders faced off again in the Tour de France, with Armstrong emerging as the overall winner once again. However, the race was marred by controversy, as several of Armstrong's teammates were implicated in a doping scandal that raised questions about the legitimacy of the team's victories.

Doping Scandals and the Legacy of the Rivalry In the years that followed, the Armstrong-Ullrich rivalry was overshadowed by a series of doping scandals that rocked the sport of cycling. Armstrong was eventually stripped of his seven Tour de France titles after he was found to have engaged in a sophisticated doping program throughout much of his career.

Ullrich, too, was implicated in a number of doping scandals, and he ultimately retired from professional cycling in 2007. While both riders achieved great success during their careers, their legacies have been tarnished by the doping scandals that surrounded them.

Despite the controversy and scandals that surrounded the Armstrong-Ullrich rivalry, it remains one of the most intense and memorable in the history of professional cycling. The two riders pushed each other to their limits, inspiring a new generation of cyclists and captivating fans around the world.

The Importance of the Tour de France in the Rivalry

The Tour de France is the most prestigious and well-known cycling race in the world, and it has played a significant role in the rivalry between Lance Armstrong and Jan Ullrich. Both cyclists had a fierce and highly publicized competition for the coveted yellow jersey, which is awarded to the winner of the Tour de France.

Origins of the Tour de France

The Tour de France was first organized in 1903 by French sports newspaper L'Auto as a way to boost circulation. The race covered a total of 2,428 kilometers over six stages, with the winner, Maurice Garin, completing the course in 94 hours and 33 minutes. The race quickly gained popularity, and by 1910, it had become an international event, with cyclists from other countries participating.

The Importance of the Tour de France in the Armstrong-Ullrich Rivalry

Lance Armstrong and Jan Ullrich were two of the most dominant cyclists of their era, and they both had their sights set on winning the Tour de France. The two cyclists faced off in several editions of the race, with Armstrong emerging as the victor on several occasions.

Armstrong's victories in the Tour de France cemented his status as one of the greatest cyclists of all time, and his success in the race was a significant factor in his rivalry with Ullrich. The two cyclists had contrasting styles of racing, with Armstrong known for his aggressive approach and Ullrich for his consistency and endurance.

The 2003 Tour de France was particularly significant for the Armstrong-Ullrich rivalry, as it marked the 100th anniversary of the race. Armstrong had won the race for the previous four years, and Ullrich was determined to break his winning streak. However, Armstrong proved too strong for Ullrich once again, winning the race by 61 seconds.

The Legacy of the Tour de France in the Armstrong-Ullrich Rivalry

The Armstrong-Ullrich rivalry has had a lasting impact on the Tour de France and the sport of cycling as a whole. Armstrong's seven consecutive victories in the race made him a legend in the sport, but his subsequent doping scandal tainted his legacy and cast a shadow over the race.

The Tour de France has since implemented stricter anti-doping measures to prevent similar scandals from occurring in the future. However, the race continues to be a major event in the cycling world, and the Armstrong-Ullrich rivalry remains one of the most memorable and significant in the race's history.

Recent Matchups and Future Prospects

Since the retirement of both Armstrong and Ullrich, the Tour de France has seen several other dominant cyclists, including Chris Froome and Tadej Pogacar. However, the race has also been marred by further doping scandals and controversy.

Looking ahead, the Tour de France and the sport of cycling as a whole face significant challenges, including improving anti-doping measures and ensuring the safety of cyclists during races. Despite these challenges, the race continues to attract the world's best cyclists, and the rivalry between Armstrong and Ullrich remains a testament to the enduring appeal of the Tour de France.

Chapter 4: Ohio State vs. Michigan in College Football

Origins of the Rivalry

The rivalry between Ohio State and Michigan is one of the oldest and most intense in college football. Dating back to 1897, the two teams have played against each other every year, except for 1918, due to the influenza pandemic, and during World War II from 1942-1945.

Origins of the Rivalry: The Ohio State-Michigan rivalry began in 1897 when Michigan was the more dominant program. Michigan had won four of the five games played between the two schools, and it looked like Ohio State would be the next victim. However, the Buckeyes pulled off a 34-0 upset victory, starting a new era of competition between the two teams.

In the early days, the rivalry was not as heated as it is today. The two teams had a friendly relationship and often shared coaching staff. For example, Ohio State's first head coach, Frederick C. "Daddy" King, played for and coached at Michigan before taking the Ohio State job.

The rivalry began to intensify in the 1930s when the two teams started competing for the Big Ten Championship. Both teams were dominating the conference, and the annual showdown between Ohio State and Michigan became the most important game of the year.

One of the most significant moments in the rivalry occurred in 1950 when Michigan's head coach, Bennie Oosterbaan, accused Ohio State of cheating. He claimed that the Buckeyes had sent spies to watch Michigan practice, which was against the rules. Ohio State denied the accusations, and the Big Ten investigated the matter, but no evidence was found. Nevertheless, the incident added fuel to the fire of the already intense rivalry.

The rivalry has continued to grow over the years, with both schools producing legendary coaches and players. Woody Hayes, Ohio State's head coach from 1951 to 1978, and Bo Schembechler, Michigan's head coach from 1969 to 1989, are two of the most iconic figures in college football history. They both had great success at their respective schools and added to the lore of the Ohio State-Michigan rivalry.

The rivalry has also been marked by some of the most memorable games in college football history. In 2006, Ohio State and Michigan were both undefeated and ranked No. 1 and No. 2 in the nation, respectively. The game, dubbed "The Game of the Century," lived up to its billing, with Ohio State winning 42-39 in a classic showdown.

In recent years, the rivalry has been dominated by Ohio State, who has won nine of the last 10 games against Michigan. Despite the recent lopsided results, the intensity and passion of the rivalry have not diminished. Every year, fans of both teams eagerly anticipate the matchup, and the game remains one of the biggest events in college football.

In conclusion, the Ohio State-Michigan rivalry has a rich and storied history, dating back over a century. What began as a friendly competition between two Midwestern schools has turned into one of the fiercest rivalries in all of sports. The rivalry has produced legendary coaches and players, epic games, and unforgettable moments, and it remains a highlight of the college football season every year.

Key Players and Memorable Moments

Ohio State vs. Michigan is one of the most storied rivalries in college football history. Over the years, there have been many great players and memorable moments that have helped define this fierce rivalry. In this section, we will take a closer look at some of the key players and memorable moments that have helped shape the Ohio State vs. Michigan rivalry.

1. Archie Griffin - Ohio State (1972-1975)

Archie Griffin is considered one of the greatest players in Ohio State history. He was a two-time Heisman Trophy winner and the only player in college football history to win the award twice. Griffin played in four Ohio State vs. Michigan games, winning three of them. In the 1973 game, he rushed for 162 yards and two touchdowns in a 10-10 tie. The following year, he rushed for 111 yards and a touchdown in a 12-10 victory over the Wolverines.

2. Charles Woodson - Michigan (1995-1997)

Charles Woodson was a standout defensive back for the Wolverines and the first primarily defensive player to win the Heisman Trophy. He played in three Ohio State vs. Michigan games, winning two of them. In the 1997 game, he intercepted a pass and returned a punt for a touchdown to help lead Michigan to a 20-14 victory. That win clinched a trip to the Rose Bowl and ultimately the national championship for the Wolverines.

3. Woody Hayes - Ohio State (1951-1978)

Woody Hayes is one of the most legendary coaches in college football history. He coached at Ohio State for 28 seasons, winning five national championships and 13 Big Ten titles. Hayes was known for his intense passion for the game and his fiery personality, which often led to memorable moments on and off the field. One of the most infamous moments in Ohio State vs. Michigan history occurred in the 1973 game, when Hayes punched a Michigan player after a late hit on the sideline.

4. Bo Schembechler - Michigan (1969-1989)

Bo Schembechler was a legendary coach at Michigan, leading the Wolverines to 13 Big Ten titles and 10 Rose Bowl appearances. He was known for his hard-nosed approach to the game and his emphasis on the running game and defense. Schembechler coached in 21 Ohio State vs. Michigan games, winning five of them. He famously said, "The greatest rivalry in all of sport is Ohio State vs. Michigan."

5. Troy Smith - Ohio State (2003-2006)

Troy Smith was a standout quarterback for Ohio State and the 2006 Heisman Trophy winner. He played in three Ohio State vs. Michigan games, winning two of them. In the

2006 game, he threw for 316 yards and four touchdowns in a 42-39 victory over the Wolverines. That win clinched a spot in the BCS National Championship game for the Buckeyes.

6. Desmond Howard - Michigan (1989-1991)

Desmond Howard was a standout wide receiver and return specialist for the Wolverines. He played in three Ohio State vs. Michigan games, winning two of them. In the 1991 game, he famously struck the Heisman Trophy pose after returning a punt for a touchdown to help lead Michigan to a 31-3 victory over the Buckeyes.

7. Jim Tressel - Ohio State (2001-2010)

Jim Tressel was the head coach at Ohio State from 2001-2010, leading the Buckeyes to seven Big Ten titles and a national championship in 2002. He coached in nine Ohio State vs. Michigan games, winning seven of them. Tressel was known for his conservative game plan, often relying on a strong defense and running game to secure victories. In the 2002 national championship season, Tressel's Buckeyes defeated Michigan 14-9 in a hard-fought battle. The game was marked by a strong defensive showing from both teams, with Ohio State's defense intercepting Michigan quarterback John Navarre four times. However, Tressel's legacy at Ohio State was tarnished when he was forced to resign in 2011 amid a scandal involving NCAA violations and improper benefits to players.

Following Tressel's departure, Urban Meyer took over as head coach at Ohio State in 2012. Meyer quickly established himself as one of the top coaches in college football, leading the Buckeyes to a national championship in 2014 and two Big Ten titles. He coached in six Ohio State vs. Michigan games, winning all six of them. Meyer's offensive-minded approach helped to revolutionize Ohio State's offense, and his teams often put up big numbers against the Wolverines. In 2018, Meyer announced his retirement from coaching, leaving behind a legacy as one of the greatest coaches in Ohio State football history.

The Impact of the Rivalry on College Football

The Ohio State vs. Michigan rivalry is one of the most storied in all of college football, with a history spanning over a century. As such, it has had a significant impact on the sport as a whole, shaping the way in which college football is played and followed.

One of the primary impacts of the rivalry has been its ability to capture the attention of fans across the country. While many rivalries exist in college football, few can match the level of intensity and national interest generated by the Ohio State vs. Michigan matchup. Year after year, the game attracts a massive audience, with millions tuning in to watch the game on television or stream it online. This has led to increased revenue for both schools and the Big Ten Conference, which uses the game as a marquee event to promote the league.

Moreover, the rivalry has also had an impact on the way in which college football is played. Both Ohio State and Michigan have a reputation for producing top-tier football programs, and their annual matchup has often been a proving ground for innovative strategies and techniques. Coaches on both sides of the rivalry have developed new tactics to try and gain an advantage over their opponents, leading to the development of new plays and formations that have since become staples of college football.

Additionally, the Ohio State vs. Michigan rivalry has played a significant role in shaping the identity of both schools. The matchup is often seen as a clash of cultures, with Ohio State representing the blue-collar work ethic of the Midwest and Michigan representing the intellectual prowess of the East Coast. This dynamic has helped to foster a sense of pride and identity among students, alumni, and fans on both sides, creating a strong sense of community around the football programs.

The rivalry has also had an impact on the careers of players and coaches involved in the matchup. The intense competition between Ohio State and Michigan has often been a proving ground for the best and brightest football talent, with many players and coaches going on to have successful careers at the college and professional levels. For example, former Ohio State head coach Urban Meyer and former Michigan head coach Lloyd Carr both had a significant impact on the rivalry during their tenures, with Meyer leading Ohio State to six victories over Michigan and Carr leading the Wolverines to a national championship in 1997.

In conclusion, the Ohio State vs. Michigan rivalry has had a profound impact on college football, from the way in which the sport is played to the way in which fans and alumni view their respective schools. Its ability to capture the national spotlight and generate intense interest has made it one of the most iconic rivalries in sports, and its impact will continue to be felt for generations to come.

Recent Matchups and Future Prospects

The Ohio State vs. Michigan rivalry has remained one of the most intense in college football, with both teams competing at the highest level each year. In recent years, the Buckeyes have been dominant, winning 17 of the last 20 meetings between the two teams. The Wolverines, however, have made strides to narrow the gap and reclaim their dominance in the series.

In the most recent matchup in 2021, Ohio State defeated Michigan 42-27. The Buckeyes had a dominant performance on offense, led by quarterback C.J. Stroud who threw for 432 yards and six touchdowns. The win secured Ohio State's spot in the Big Ten Championship game and further cemented their status as one of the top teams in college football.

Looking ahead to the future, both Ohio State and Michigan are poised to continue their success on the gridiron. The Buckeyes have consistently been one of the top programs in the country and are expected to continue to compete for conference and national championships. Michigan, on the other hand, has undergone some changes in recent years with the hiring of head coach Jim Harbaugh in 2015. While the Wolverines have not yet been able to match Ohio State's success, they have made improvements under Harbaugh's leadership and are hopeful for continued success in the future.

Another factor that could impact the future of the rivalry is the potential expansion of the college football playoff. If the playoff were to expand to include more teams, it could provide an opportunity for both Ohio State and Michigan to compete for a national championship even if they don't win their conference. This could add even more excitement and intensity to the rivalry and create new opportunities for both teams to assert their dominance on the national stage.

In addition to on-field success, the rivalry between Ohio State and Michigan continues to have a significant impact off the field as well. The annual matchup between the two teams is one of the most highly anticipated games in all of college football, drawing national attention and attracting fans from all over the country. The game also has significant economic implications for both universities and the surrounding communities, with millions of dollars in revenue generated each year.

Overall, the future of the Ohio State vs. Michigan rivalry looks bright, with both teams poised to continue their success on the field and create new memories for fans and alumni alike. The intense competition between these two programs is what makes college football so exciting, and it's a rivalry that will continue to captivate fans for years to come.

The Role of Coaches in the Rivalry

The Ohio State vs. Michigan rivalry is not just about the players on the field, but also about the coaches who lead them. Throughout the history of the rivalry, several coaches have played a significant role in shaping its direction and intensity.

One of the most iconic coaches in the rivalry is Woody Hayes, who was the head coach at Ohio State from 1951-1978. Hayes was known for his intense hatred of Michigan and famously said, "I would rather beat Michigan than go to heaven." During his tenure at Ohio State, Hayes led the Buckeyes to 13 Big Ten titles and five national championships. He also coached in 17 Ohio State vs. Michigan games, winning 11 of them.

On the Michigan side, Bo Schembechler was one of the most influential coaches in the rivalry. Schembechler was the head coach at Michigan from 1969-1989 and had a record of 194-48-5. He coached in 21 Ohio State vs. Michigan games, winning five of them. Schembechler's teams were known for their toughness and physicality, and he often clashed with Hayes on the field.

Another notable coach in the rivalry is Jim Tressel, who was the head coach at Ohio State from 2001-2010. Tressel had a record of 9-1 against Michigan and led the

Buckeyes to six Big Ten titles and a national championship in 2002. Tressel's tenure at Ohio State was marked by controversy, as he was forced to resign in 2011 due to a scandal involving players trading memorabilia for tattoos.

On the Michigan side, Jim Harbaugh is the current head coach and has been in the position since 2015. Harbaugh was a former quarterback for Michigan and played in three Ohio State vs. Michigan games during his college career. As a coach, Harbaugh has a record of 1-4 against Ohio State, and his teams have struggled to keep pace with the Buckeyes in recent years.

The rivalry between Ohio State and Michigan has also seen its fair share of coaching controversies. In 2011, Ohio State coach Urban Meyer was accused of covering up a scandal involving one of his players, which ultimately led to his suspension for three games in 2018. In 2013, Michigan fired head coach Brady Hoke after four seasons, during which the team struggled to compete with Ohio State and other top programs.

Despite the controversies, the coaches in the Ohio State vs. Michigan rivalry have played a crucial role in shaping its history and intensity. Their passion and dedication to their respective programs have inspired generations of players and fans, and their legacies will continue to be felt for years to come.

Conclusion
The Evolution of Red War Rivalries in Sports

Introduction: Throughout the world of sports, there are numerous rivalries that have become legendary in their intensity and passion. From the New York Yankees vs. Boston Red Sox in baseball to the Ohio State vs. Michigan in college football, these rivalries have captured the imagination of fans worldwide. In this chapter, we will explore the evolution of these red war rivalries in sports, looking at how they have developed over time and the factors that have contributed to their enduring popularity.

Origins of Red War Rivalries: Red war rivalries have their origins in the tribalism of human society, where groups would compete against each other for resources and survival. In the modern era, these rivalries have taken on a more symbolic role, representing the cultural and regional differences between teams and their fans. The origins of these rivalries can often be traced back to historical events, such as battles or disputes, that have taken on a mythical status within the collective consciousness of the fanbase.

The Role of Media in the Evolution of Red War Rivalries: The advent of mass media has played a significant role in the evolution of red war rivalries in sports. Television broadcasts, radio shows, and newspapers have all contributed to the promotion and perpetuation of these rivalries, creating a sense of drama and excitement that draws fans in. The rise of social media has also allowed fans to connect with each other and with their teams in ways that were previously impossible, further fueling the intensity of these rivalries.

The Impact of Red War Rivalries on Players: Red war rivalries can have a significant impact on the players involved, both on and off the field. The pressure of representing their team in these high-stakes matchups can be immense, and the emotions that come with a win or a loss can be overwhelming. Players may also find themselves the subject of intense scrutiny and criticism from the media and fans, adding to the pressure they already face.

The Cultural Significance of Red War Rivalries: Red war rivalries are not just about sports; they are about culture, identity, and belonging. They reflect the values and beliefs of the communities that support them, and they have become an essential part of the social fabric of those communities. For many fans, these rivalries are more than just games; they are a way of life, a source of pride, and a symbol of their identity.

The Future of Red War Rivalries: As sports continue to evolve, so too will the nature of red war rivalries. New rivalries may emerge as teams and fanbases shift and change, and old rivalries may fade away as the cultural landscape evolves. However, the enduring popularity of these rivalries suggests that they will continue to be an integral part of the sports world for years to come.

Conclusion: Red war rivalries in sports are a reflection of the human need for competition, tribalism, and identity. They have evolved over time, driven by factors such as media, culture, and historical events, and have become an essential part of the social fabric of the communities that support them. While the future of these rivalries is uncertain, one thing is clear: their enduring popularity and impact on sports and culture ensure that they will continue to be a source of passion and excitement for fans around the world.

The Importance of Fans and Media in Fostering Rivalries

Sports rivalries are often a product of geography, history, and cultural differences, but they are sustained and intensified by the passion of fans and the attention of the media. In this section, we will explore the critical role that fans and media play in fostering and shaping sports rivalries.

Fans are an essential element of sports rivalries, providing the emotional fuel that drives the intensity of the competition. Rivalries bring together communities of fans who share a common love for their team and a shared hatred for their opponents. Fans are the ones who create the chants, the banners, the taunts, and the traditions that make sports rivalries so memorable. They are the ones who show up in force to pack the stadium, and they are the ones who fuel the online conversations and debates that rage on social media platforms.

Media coverage is another critical factor in the development and sustenance of sports rivalries. The media not only provides a platform for fans to follow and discuss their teams, but it also shapes the narrative and discourse around rivalries. The media can amplify the intensity of a rivalry by highlighting the history, culture, and personalities involved. They can also play a significant role in fueling tensions by creating drama, spreading rumors, and stirring up controversy. The media can also provide a platform for fans to interact with each other and with their teams, further reinforcing the emotional attachment to the rivalry.

Moreover, the media can contribute to the commercialization of sports rivalries, turning them into lucrative products for sports leagues and media companies. Rivalries generate significant revenue through increased ticket sales, merchandise sales, and advertising revenue. Sports leagues and media companies capitalize on this by promoting and marketing rivalries to maximize profits. This commercialization can both enhance and detract from the authenticity and intensity of rivalries.

In recent years, social media has emerged as a new and powerful force in the world of sports rivalries. Social media platforms provide fans with new ways to engage with their teams and with each other, fueling conversations, debates, and taunts in real-time. Social media has also provided a platform for players and coaches to interact with fans, further intensifying the emotional attachment to the rivalry. At the same time, social media can also exacerbate tensions and create conflicts, as fans can use these platforms to harass and bully players and coaches, creating negative consequences for the athletes involved.

In conclusion, fans and media are integral to the development and sustenance of sports rivalries. Fans bring the passion, emotion, and traditions that define rivalries, while the media provides the platform and narrative that shapes the discourse around these contests. The relationship between fans, media, and rivalries is complex and dynamic, with each influencing the other in different ways. Understanding the role that fans and media play in sports rivalries can provide valuable insights into the nature and evolution of these contests and can help us appreciate the cultural and social significance of sports in our lives.

The Future of Red War Rivalries in a Changing Sports Landscape

Introduction: Red War rivalries have been an integral part of the sports world for decades, captivating fans and igniting passions that often extend beyond the playing field. However, with the ever-changing sports landscape and the rise of new forms of entertainment, the future of these rivalries is uncertain. In this section, we will discuss the challenges that Red War rivalries face and examine the potential future of these intense sporting competitions.

Challenges facing Red War Rivalries: One of the major challenges facing Red War rivalries is the changing sports landscape. With the rise of new sports, such as esports and mixed martial arts, traditional sports may struggle to maintain their relevance and popularity. Additionally, the emergence of social media and the ease of access to information mean that fans have more options than ever before, making it harder to capture their attention.

Another challenge is the changing nature of sports fandom. Younger generations may not have the same attachment to the traditional Red War rivalries as older fans, which could lead to a decline in interest and attendance. Furthermore, the commercialization of sports, with more focus on revenue and profit, may diminish the authenticity and passion of these rivalries.

Future of Red War Rivalries: Despite the challenges, Red War rivalries are likely to remain a fixture in the sports world. The intense emotions and deep-seated loyalties that drive these competitions are unlikely to disappear overnight. However, to remain relevant, these rivalries must adapt to the changing sports landscape and fan preferences.

One potential avenue for the future of Red War rivalries is to embrace new technology and media platforms. Social media and streaming services can provide new ways for fans to engage with these rivalries, from virtual watch parties to interactive fan experiences. By utilizing these tools, Red War rivalries can expand their reach and appeal to a broader audience.

Another approach is to focus on the cultural significance of these rivalries. As we have seen in the chapters above, Red War rivalries often have deep historical and cultural roots. By emphasizing these aspects, sports organizations can tap into a broader audience that is interested in the history and traditions of these rivalries. Additionally, by promoting the positive aspects of these rivalries, such as community pride and sportsmanship, Red

War rivalries can attract new fans who are drawn to these values.

Conclusion: In conclusion, the future of Red War rivalries is uncertain, but there are steps that can be taken to ensure their longevity and relevance. By embracing new technology, emphasizing the cultural significance of these rivalries, and promoting positive values, Red War rivalries can continue to captivate fans and inspire intense emotions for years to come. While there are challenges ahead, the passion and loyalty that drive these rivalries are unlikely to fade away any time soon.

The Impact of Globalization on Red War

The impact of globalization on red war rivalries in sports cannot be overlooked. With the advent of technology and the growth of social media, fans and players are now more connected than ever before. As a result, rivalries have transcended national borders and have become global in nature. This has both positive and negative implications for red war rivalries.

On the positive side, globalization has allowed fans from different parts of the world to connect and engage with each other over their shared passion for a particular sport or rivalry. This has led to the formation of global fan communities that can rally behind their respective teams, no matter where they are playing. This has also led to an increase in the popularity of red war rivalries outside of their home countries, leading to greater exposure for the sport and the teams involved.

However, globalization has also led to the commercialization of sports, where the emphasis is placed on profits over the traditions and values that underpin red war rivalries. As a result, many fans feel that the authenticity and passion of red war rivalries are being diluted, with corporate interests taking priority over the interests of the fans.

Moreover, globalization has also led to an increase in the mobility of players, with players moving between different teams and leagues more frequently than in the past. This has led to a decrease in player loyalty and a weakening of red war rivalries, as players may not feel the same attachment to a particular team or rivalry as fans do.

In addition, globalization has also brought about changes in the way that sports are consumed and experienced. With the rise of streaming services and social media, fans can now watch matches from different parts of the world in real-time, leading to a decrease in the importance of physical proximity to a particular team or rivalry.

Despite these challenges, it is important to recognize that red war rivalries are not static, and they have evolved over time. As such, it is important for fans, players, and stakeholders to adapt and embrace the changes brought about by globalization in order to ensure that red war rivalries continue to thrive in the future.

In conclusion, the impact of globalization on red war rivalries in sports has been significant, both positive and negative. While it has led to an increase in the popularity of rivalries outside of their home countries and has allowed fans from different parts of the world to connect and engage with each other, it has also led to the commercialization of sports and a decrease in player loyalty. It is important for stakeholders to adapt to these changes and find ways to ensure that red war rivalries continue to thrive in a changing sports landscape.

THE END

Key Terms and Definitions

To help you better understand the language and concepts related to aging and older adults, below you will find a list of key terms and their definitions.

1. Sports Rivalry - A competitive relationship between two or more teams or individuals in a particular sport, characterized by a long-standing history of intense competition, animosity, and hostility.

2. Red War - A term used to describe sports rivalries that are marked by intense emotions, high stakes, and a sense of cultural, regional, or national pride.

3. Fan Psychology - The study of the psychological and emotional factors that motivate sports fans to support and identify with their favorite teams and athletes.

4. Social Identity Theory - A psychological theory that explains how individuals form a sense of identity and self-esteem through their membership in social groups, including sports teams and fan communities.

5. In-Group Bias - A cognitive bias that leads individuals to favor and defend their own group over other groups, even when there is no logical or rational basis for doing so.

6. Intergroup Conflict - A type of conflict that arises between two or more social groups, based on perceived differences in values, beliefs, and goals.

7. Media Framing - The process by which media outlets shape and influence public perception of sports events and rivalries, by selectively highlighting certain aspects of the competition and downplaying others.

8. National Identity - The sense of belonging and shared cultural heritage that individuals feel as members of a particular nation or country.

9. Doping Scandals - The use of performance-enhancing drugs in sports, which can lead to disqualification, sanctions, and loss of credibility for athletes and teams.

10. Globalization - The process by which economic, cultural, and social exchanges and interactions take place between different countries and regions, leading to the spread of ideas, values, and practices across national boundaries.

Supporting Materials

Introduction:

- Feinberg, R. (2008). Red Sox Nation? Exploring the size, scope, and power of Red Sox Nation. Journal of Sports Media, 3(1), 79-98.

Chapter 1: New York Yankees vs. Boston Red Sox in Baseball:

- Stout, G. (2005). Yankees vs. Red Sox: The endless rivalry. Houghton Mifflin Harcourt.

- Stout, G. (2017). The selling of the Babe: The deal that changed baseball and created a legend. Thomas Dunne Books.

Chapter 2: Brazil vs. Argentina in Soccer:

- Goldblatt, D. (2014). Futebol Nation: A Footballing History of Brazil. Penguin Books.

- Murray, B. (2014). The world's game: A history of soccer. University of Illinois Press.

Chapter 3: Armstrong vs. Ullrich in Cycling:

- Bill, S. (2012). Tour de France: The history, the legend, the riders. Quercus.

- Coyle, D. (2004). Lance Armstrong's war: One man's battle against fate, fame, love, death, scandal, and a few other rivals on the road to the Tour de France. HarperCollins.

Chapter 4: Ohio State vs. Michigan in College Football:

- Bacon, J. (2011). Three and out: Rich Rodriguez and the Michigan Wolverines in the crucible of college football. Farrar, Straus and Giroux.
- Davis, J. H. (2018). Let's Go!: The History of the 29th Infantry Division 1917-2001. Turner Publishing Company.

Conclusion:

- McGuire, J. (2014). The history of Western civilization in sports. McFarland & Company, Inc., Publishers.
- Rorabaugh, W. J. (2012). Sports in American history: From colonization to globalization. University of Illinois Press.

www.ingramcontent.com/pod-product-compliance
Lightning Source LLC
LaVergne TN
LVHW012125070526
838202LV00056B/5862